It Will Be

An Anthology Relating to

The Black Experience

Exhale Publishing

Published in 2021 by Exhale Publishing

Copyright © Exhale Publishing

Exhale Publishing is part of 4D-House Ltd.

4D HOUSE

Prepared for publishing by Careen Latoya Lawrence
Editor: Olivia Newnham
Photographer: Henrique J Paris

The author or authors assert their moral right under the Copyright , Designs and Patent Act, 1988, to be identified as the author or authors of this work.

All Rights reserved. No part of this publication may be reproduced, copied, stored in a retrieval system, or transmitted, in any form or by any means, without the prior written consent of the copyright holder, nor be otherwise circulated in any form of binding or cover other than that in which it is published and without a similar condition being imposed on the subsequent purchaser.

A CIP catalogue record for this title is available from the British Library.

Preface

2020 was the year the world changed considerably for each of us. Plans made to last us for the year had to be cancelled, and formats for events were altered. This book, It Will Be, started as an event which was to be inclusive of poetry and art; however, with Covid taking the world by storm, we had to postpone the events. We had to pull all the pieces together in a book, the step which had to come before it's time.

The pieces you will come across are all around one central theme, The Black Experience. Each poet was given a subtheme to which they wrote new poems, or pieces they had previously written. At the beginning of each section you will be introduced to each poet to allow you to know a little bit more about them. I must extend my thanks to each of them for sharing their art and heart beyond the stage.

There are six themes which you will be presented with, all in order of when the event was to occur. The first event which we did manage to host, took place on Saturday 15th February, to be followed by the next event in April on Saturday 18th and so on.

I hope you can resonate with at least one of the pieces within the book, and, can find strength within at least one of the pieces.

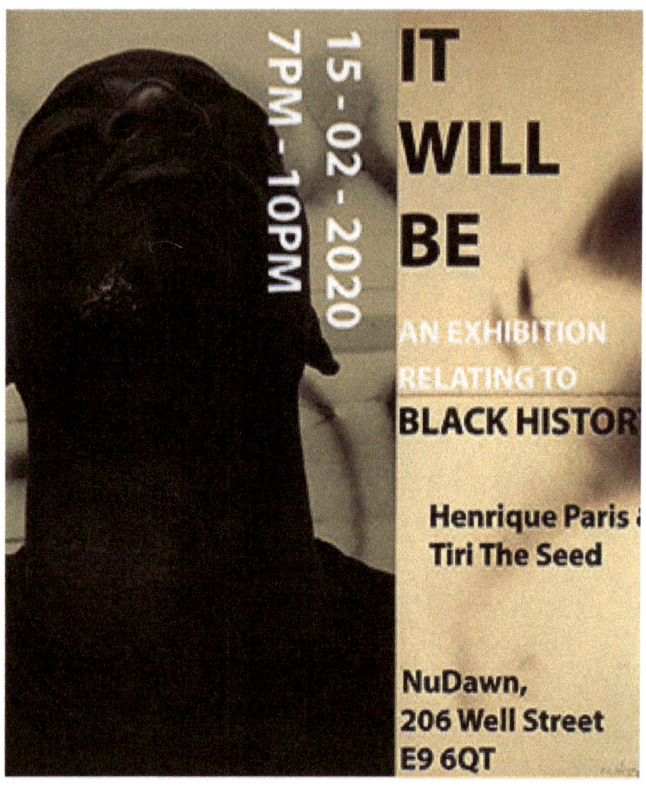

What you see here is the flyer which had been created by Henrique Paris who had taken part in the first and only exhibition we had before Covid-19 set in and reared its head. It was an absolute pleasure having Henrique along sharing his photography in relation to Black History. There are moments in life which ought to be cherished and this was wone of them. We at 4D-House Ltd. couldn't have asked for more.

I would like to extend thanks to Henrique for allowing me to use his photograph for the cover of the book. It only felt right to have the cover as close to the flyer as possible, knowing that this was the beginning of the journey you will venture on.

Content

Black History
Tiri The Seed
- Just Cos We Know Street
- Mama and Baba
- Mansa Musa I of Mali
- Africa

Interactions with Blacks
Alex Otubanjo
- My Homeland
- Colourism Chronicles
- This Was Never a Place for Us
- University Storytelling (As An Ethnic Minority)
- What I Would Tell My Daughter

Black Bodies
Aaron Daniel
- Grand Rising
- Untitled
- Branches
- Molala Trees
- IMAX

Black Hands
Solomon Adams
- 1
- 2
- 3
- 4
- 5

Black Mental Health
Sami Rhymes
- Talking About the Pain
- Interracial Therapy
- Being Black's a Crime
- Black Don't Crack

Dynamics in the Black Family
Georgia Moona-Sam
Toxicity in the Black Community

The Poets

Tiri The Seed

Aaron Daniel

Sami Rhymes

Alex Otubanjo

Solomon Adams

Georgia Moona-Sam

Black History

It Will Be: Black History was the only event we were able to have in 2020 though they were all mapped out and ready for us to go. It was a lesson, no matter how well prepared you are for something, plans can and will change due to circumstances beyond your control.

The event took place at NuDawn found in East London. What's more than a Black event taking part in a Black-owned space?

On the night we had Tiri as the poet and Henrique J Paris as the photographer. The brief they got was a simple one, share pieces which they felt represented how they view the way Black History shapes us today and how future generation will be affected by today's events.

On the next page you'll find out more about Tiri, so I'll use this page to give you a little background information about Henrique.

Henrique is a young multi-disciplinary artist who, for his photography, uses film cameras. You remember the cameras we had before digital cameras. The ones you'd need to take the film to a shop to get the photos developed? That's the kind of camera he uses, and he gets some of the most amazing shots.

The photo on the front cover and page (ii) is one he took, which he also used to design the flyer.

It was a pleasure having Henrique on board sharing his art with us and explaining some of his photography with us.

We only hope for the world to re-open once again for us to be able to finish off what we started last February. For now, please enjoy the poetry.

Black History

<u>Tiri The Seed</u>

Spoken Word Poet, Rapper and all-round creative, Tiri has done work for BT Sport, Enterprise Rent-a-Car, HSBC and featured on BBC Radio London.

With Dynamic word play, Smooth flows and Fearless content. He has performed and numerous shows and Spoken Word events across the capital. Recently has just released his first single called Le Struggle which is available to stream on all major platforms. Very active on social media, behind his fundamental idea of Sow the Seed, there is still a lot of room for growth.

Just 'Cos We Know Street

Just 'cos we know street,
Doesn't mean that we road.

Yeah, we know the code.
It's like an equation
Embedded within
The codec of our skin,
The physical manifestation
Which can be simplified as postal.
Decades of segregation in
Depreciating accommodation.

Zero ownership
Means you will fight
For the zero that you have .
I will always love my parents for what they did,
But they never had it
Quite like us as kids.
The conditions of change as the years grew older.
Something about the foreign winter

Just seemed to hit colder.
They came with plan
On a minimum promise of work
An ethic instilled in us
Often misrepresented.
Our cultures began to mix,
Our heritage different but not distant.
African and Caribbean,

The sauce started mixing,
Same pot but the flavour was not the same.
Can you have a clash of cultures
When the two originate from the same?
To us it's obvious,
But to others
It's like looking at two pieces of paper
That are plain.

We had to empower ourselves with new knowledge
Build it into our structure.
As the era begins to change,
We need a new infrastructure.
Now can we be blamed for chasing conditions?
Our physical and mental conditions,
Not determined by the conditions
Of the environment we live in?

Like why do so many have to die for our rights
 So I'd have the right to write this verse
But when we celebrate which is in our nature,
Wverybody wants to be diverse?
Our naturally welcoming nature
Means there is no going back
Once you experience our flavour.
The sensation of flavour

Perceived by new tongues that we introduced,
You could call it the fresh taste.
How many times have you had a friend over
 At your mums and said "try this"?
It's not exclusive to race
'Cos I remember I went over to my friend Lee's
And it was the first time I tried
Rice and peas not born of an African hand.

We started to develop a new colloquial slang
That was a rejection of the system,
 its teachings,
And the man.
This isn't anything new.
 When you feel marginalised,
You start to see the world with marginal eyes.
It became so coded our parents couldn't understand.

This was our broken English,
We weren't broken
Yet we were broke in England.
Big doses of Caribbean,

rhyming slang,
Seasoned with African flavour
 with a sprinkle of Americanisms to add texture.
A simple nod and wagwan
Now our universal greeting.
And yeah, we can be loud
And we like to celebrate our wins,
Getting defensive over the little that's ours,

But, when you've lived
A life time in a garden
That has never seen flowers
And one finally grows,
You'll give your life before
You let anybody come and take.

One word on the authorities:
Your prejudice poisons everyone's minds.

I've been arrested one time,
I committed no crime,
I was just a Black face in the wrong place,
The street I lived on.
Africans,
Caribbeans,
And few of my White dons
Mixed in a way that created a wave for us.

Now just because you don't speak like us
Doesn't mean we on cruddy activities.

Just because we know street,
Doesn't mean that we road.

Mama and Baba

The air is brisk,
The wind bites,
And the Sun hides.
This is nothing like home.

The Air smells different
And I've never seen so many white people in one place.
I've never been the odd one out before,
There is something about the way they look at my face.

We came here to be free,
So our minds we'll set free.
Ready to work hard
And they will educate me.

This will be a shock to the system culturally.
A system in shock will breed a new culture city.
We will be the pioneers
Discovering already discovered lands,

Do it the way they taught us.
Don't fight the beast with bare hands
But tactfully infiltrate, unite, and instigate.
Take the little you need to survive

And make sure Africa sees some of your plate.

We will carve a new life for ourselves,
This is just the beginning.
Our sons and daughters
Will speak of our bravery to take this chance

And what a chance these are
Real opportunities
And don't consider the Commonwealth unity.
This is a chance to improve
The common wealth of our community.

The risk weighs heavy on our hearts,
but failure doesn't enter the realm of possibility,
not even potentially or possibly.
We are going to pave the way
for all those who want to follow us.
We are going to pave the way
for all those who want to follow us.

I look at my parents and I get it,
Mama and Baba,
I totally get it.
You saw your dreams in the world
and you went to go get it.

Talk about going into the unknown,
knowingly going to a place not known by many
and saying bye to what you know...

Home.

Hunting treasure that can't be held
like trying to catch smoke.
The Lord was thy shepherd,
the fuel thy hope.
When the burden of glory is heavy,
but the light shines so bright
the sacrifices you made hold the most value.
It's about more than just a better you,
a better one,
a better two.
You might not be able to see the path,
but the Lord was guiding you through
as if the future was screened to you in private
and not for every man.

Not every man will know what you sacrificed.

They accessed Africa's riches,
now we must access their education.

They think we're weak,
but we will show them strength.
They will throw sticks and hit us with malicious intent.
Our vison will remain true
our intentions pure.
They will see Black excellence.

Mansa Musa I of Mali

Musa Keita, to me I'm just Musa.
It's true that my blood line is full of prestige,
but to me I'm just Musa Keita.

It's true,
my Great Uncle Sundiata Keita is the founder
of the foundations that founded this Mali Empire
that I have elevated to greatness.

Let it be known it was not my blood line
that decreed me next in line
but the line of our Hierarchy is nominated
by he who stood before as ruler.

I stepped into something good
but history only remembers the great.
The building blocks are in place.
The work will be tireless,
but for time we must not wait.

The Europeans fight each other,
and we will let them wage war against themselves.
The Motherland will provide for us as is our nature.
The nurture she gives us is our source of riches.
They don't realise it yet
but it's what makes us the richest,
but ritual must never be disregarded.

Pilgrimage to Mecca is an absolute
that I will absolutely undertake
with the greatest pride.
No expense shall be spared,
and wealth shall be shared
as a man is only as wealthy as those around him.

My servants shall be dressed in the finest Persian silk.
The entire entourage will be adorned
in the gold and riches of our land.

This is not for show as I plan to show
the opulent beauty of our home
is for the many and not the few.
A redistribution if you will,
giving back to those who give it up for you.
For a true leader,
this is an easy task without question.

But yet there is always the question,
some will say
I spent lavish
and my extravagance caused inflation
in the Mediterranean
when in truth, what they don't like
is that I shared my wealth.
It is said that I am the only instance in History
when one man controlled the price of Gold,
Trust me I had that Drip Drip.

Now it's important to understand
wealth can never be the mark of a man.
There is a plan;
Senegal, Mauritania, Ivory Coast, Burkina Faso,
Niger, Gambia, Guinea, and Guinea Bissau,
all along the Niger River.
A present-day reflection of my Empire's presence.
The boarders of my rule
extended to all these tenants.

Gold made us rich,
but the wealth is in mastery of self.
I said the work would be tireless.

Mosques will be built in Goa, Djenne, and Timbuktu.
By the grace of Allah,
they will stand the test of time.

The University of Sankore will provide
knowledge for all those who seek to learn.
If you build it,
they will come long after my flame has burned.

A Spiritual home now,
it's a centre of education
rich in trade.
Merchants come from far and wide.
Our people have Gold
they know they'll get paid.

I have been known in my time as Emir of Melle,
Conqueror of Ghanata,
Lord of the mines of Wangara,
Lord of Mali,
Kankan Musa,
The Richest man to ever exist,
King of Kings.

I am Mansa Musa I of Mali.

Africa

If you want to talk about history
then you have to watch the time past
as often his story is told by he who victorious.
So, what does that mean?
It means we don't tell our own stories.

Our trauma is delivered to us
on a cold plate of glory
with the feelings attached
that we're supposed to feel; grateful.
Are we just supposed to ok with this?
The deception has become see through.
But we were always taught
never bite the hand that feeds you.
Such conflict and contrast of emotions.
How can I love the place I live,
when the atrocities of history in the place I live,
didn't consider people that look like me
as human?

Misconception and misrepresentation
have continued to this day
Instead of showing adverts for charity case
starving African children,
claiming Africa to be poor, destitute,
Let's remember almost one-third of children in
the UK currently live in poverty.
You should really learn to dance at yard
before you dance abroad.

We will never forget the 40 million Africans
dating back the 16th century
forced into slavery and lost to human brutality.
We will never forget the race for Africa
or how Europeans colonised our land
claiming it for their own.
but when we move to Europe seeking opportunities
we're the ones told to go home.

I'm sick of it,
I'm sick of this being all that we're taught
we leave school with such a poor school of thought.

Even at this big age,
some one in their mid to late 20's
once asked me if Africa had any cities?
I was blown away not by the ignorance
but by the power of misrepresentation,
not just of a nation but of the entire continent.

So, where were we before them
and who are we really then?
What is the truth about Black history?
Mansa Musa started our journey off exquisitely,
let's call the glory on the Western front.

So, let's move into Central Sahara
the Empire of Kanem Borno
where the Seifuwa dynasty ruled
from 1075AD until the 1800s.
With multi storey buildings that told multiple stories
and a saloon bar
that looked like it came from the Wild West.
I wonder how many heads got dash out
for having one too many?

Let's travel South to an area close to my heart,
The portion ruled by the Munhumutapa,
we're talking Mozambique, South Africa,
and my beloved Zimbabwe.
The home of the family tree that Tiri The Seed fell from.

The cultural capital of Munhumutapa
was Great Zimbabwe where the ruins still stand.
Bricks made to hold with no mortar,
foundations built to last the test of time.
Rich with gold, these medieval Africans
were able to mine 43 and a quarter million tons Gold ore
producing 700 tons of pure Gold,

that's real medieval industry.
To put that into perspective
a single ton of pure Gold has a current value
of $64.3 Million dollars,
I think its safe to say all my guys are ballers.

Did you know Ethiopian literally translates to
those of burnt face?
And very often how those outside our land
referred to out woman and man.
A non-offensive term and it's only right we portioned it
to a piece of land.
They built stele and Obelisks between 300BC to 300AD
They were one of only four nations allowed to issue coins
made of Gold.

It is home to St Mary of Zion Cathedral,
one of the oldest Christian Cathedrals on Earth.
The Lord has been with us from the Jump.

The Swahili Confederation
stretched over Somalia, Kenya, Zanzibar, and Tanzania.
With impressive architecture,
they produce steel for over 2000 years.

The Ancient Greeks witnessed
true rulers of the Nile Valley.
Herodotus said they are dark skinned with woolly hair.
I don't think we can be confused
about who the Nile really belonged to.
We came from the beginning of the Nile
where the God-Hapi dwells,
at the foot hills of the Mountains of the Moon,
from the Ancient Nubian super city South Kerma.
Then the most powerful Kushite ,Pharaoh Taharqa
ruling Kush, Egypt, Syria, and Spain in his time,
and we all know about Ancient Egypt.
The fact remains,
their pyramids are the youngest in a long line
of African Architecture and unexplained brilliance.

All of the above happened
before a single European set foot on African soil.
Your bloodline is built of the back of Excellence,
don't ever let anyone else tell you
about where you came from
because you came from the start of modern evolution.
So now it's time to mould your evolution.
Adjust your mindset and rearrange your circumstances.

All that is left is growth.

Now you know where you come from,
you'll know where to go.

Interactions with Blacks

At the beginning of lockdown, mid-March 2020, we had to make the call, contact the venue and all who were to be involved and let them know it would be postponed.

Personally, I was looking forward to this one. I wanted to see what the artist would have done with the theme, and how many works he would have been able to curate for it.

To this day, I am amazed at how we all take themes and produce a wide variety of work based on what had been given.

The poet for this theme was Alex Otubanjo. I came across her work on The Black Verse's YouTube channel and believed she would have done well with this theme. I am quite pleased with the work she has produced and am certain, you, like myself, will enjoy them.

The thing about Interactions with Blacks, as you will see from Alex's pieces, it's not only to do with the way we are treated by the police. It's about how we are treated in the education system, the teachers who directly interact with us and those who indirectly interact with us.

One thing I've found difficult to do, is explaining my personal experiences with non-Blacks, especially when it has come to the way I've been treated in the work place.

If you aren't a Black individual and you are reading this, I hope you are able to understand that bit more how negative interactions impact us.

If you are a Black individual reading this, I hope you find strength in knowing that you too can make it through. We, have all been affected in some form, but, we can all make it through.

Interactions with Blacks

Alex Otubanjo

Alex Otubanjo is currently working as a Programmes Fellow with One Young World, a non-profit organisation which gathers global young leaders from around the world to tackle crucial global issues.

Alex is an alumni of Warwick University, graduating in July 2018 with a first class in Politics and International Studies. She also gained a first in her dissertation, which analysed the Black Lives Matter movement in relation to race and biopolitics. She then studied for a Masters in Global Governance and Ethics at University College London where she graduated with a Merit in September 2019.

Her passion for youth mentorship led her to becoming a Student Ambassador at Warwick, engaging with thousands of students at Widening Participation fairs across London and the West Midlands. For two years, she mentored talented Year 8 and Year 9 pupils through the Warwick Sutton Scholars Programme, through the Sutton Trust. Between 2017-2019, Alex was the Deputy Chair of the Ernst & Young (EY) Foundation's National Youth Panel for the School to Work campaign – a role centred around helping young peoples' transition from school to the workplace.

Alex was named one of the Top 150 Future Leaders in the United Kingdom of African and Caribbean descent for 2019/2020, having been recognised for her work in Widening Participation and youth mentorship.

Additionally, Alex is also a spoken word poet and has performed in places such as the British Museum and Chatham House. She created her own website "Lex-Expresses" to document her poetry - writing on themes such as child marriage, politics, identity and race.

My Homeland

My homeland is mine
but most times I only feel like a visitor.

Although I'm a woman, of Nigerian descent,
I feel my domestic and ethnic realities are dissimilar.

Even though I'm Nigerian,
when I tell people my name
I feel as if they look straight into me and say
'you fraud. You lie.
You might like Afrobeats but you're not Nigerian,
you're just a non-black person in disguise.
No, no, no,
Alex isn't and can't even be your 'real' name
because your face doesn't match the description
and your skin tone
it's not ascribed with other Alex's in the system'
and so I retreat back to my place of criticisms
and my heart stiffens.

My homeland is mine
but most times I only feel like a visitor.

With the language I struggle
and when I struggle I wish things were simpler.

It's a thing where I dread trips back to the motherland
because I know I cannot speak the mother tongue.
For a child who struggled to string words together,
and didn't speak at all
until she was required to in the classroom,
being able to speak like this
is a blessing
that not even those therapists could consume.

On every trip out, my voice is banned
so every Nigerian around me
does not struggle to understand

and for every aunty that scanned me
conceived Westernisation as a termination of my culture,
a failure to understand my identity.

Identity is a necessity.
But without being able to speak my mother tongue,
how can they even begin to respect or understand me?

My homeland is mine
but it could never be
because the knowledge of my homeland
I struggle to impart.

Like Chinua Achebe,
I'm falling apart.
I struggle to identify
with the identity given to me at the start.
It's easy to put blame on your parents
because of knowledge they failed to impart,
or yourself for immersing into the Eurocentric culture
you and your friends watch,
but as we remain 'lost in translation'
between those of the nation
and those living outside it, in isolation,
how does this expect to change?

My homeland might not be mine at this present moment,
But it will always be mine and that has never changed.

I am the daughter of parents who migrated
from this fine land,
but they ingrained and explained knowledge
so that I am chained to my dialect
despite the distance and the different customs
to our homeland we still feel the 'African connect'.

My homeland is divine.

You might read in the news
that it's in decline,

economic downturns,
gender oppression,
constant undermining,
but to me, my homeland is on the rise.
To deny its rich history and potential is a malign reality.

My homeland is rich.

Not just in resources
but also the vast range of stories,
cultures and languages that exist
There is no limit to my homeland.

My homeland is mine.

It's not defined by colonialism or conquest.
It's not defined by slavery or neglect.
It's not defined by oppression or disrespect.

My homeland has progressed,
Mother Africa.
My homeland has positive prospects.

My homeland is mine.

Colourism Chronicles

'I wish I was lighter.'
'I love my skin, but I wish my melanin was brighter.'
'I wish my skin tone was a little bit "whiter".'
I've heard some black girls say.

The worrying thing is that at their age,
they have internalised the idea of desirability
they feel is compromised by their race
and their face.
It's a shame that they feel,
at their tender age,
they're not worthy of the male gaze
because their "blackness" isn't the right shade.
So they feel dismayed,
ashamed,
and as a result, this perpetuates their psyche,
and has them wishing that they were a different shade.

'I wish I was lighter.'
'I love my skin, but I wish my melanin was brighter.'
'I wish my skin tone was a little bit "whiter".'
I've heard some black girls say.

Some of these harmful interactions
occurred in childhood.
It's a shame.
At the point where you are meant to be
innocent and carefree,
you're at a critical juncture of your young womanhood.
Most of our experiences have been marked
by irresponsible nicknames,
remarks that would have caused them
a great deal of pain

"You're blick,
bright pink lipgloss wouldn't suit a girl like you."
"Why is your skin colour like this?
It's really dirty, it looks like poo."

These school insults then sadly continue
when you enter the dating pool;
"I like my girls black, but not too dark, like the moon."
"If she's darker than this bit of charcoal,
then please return to sender,
I didn't sign up to date someone who resembles a prune."

...and so these experiences,
shutdowns,
disses have continued
From the moment you have left the womb,
left to face the world
and those who have dissed you.

Oh, how much amazing it must feel

to simply ask a black woman to undo
all these directed attacks
for something she can't control,
and to make her skin tone such a taboo.

Can you imagine how overwhelming it is

When a black woman is left with all these scars,
but are then expected to forget them
the minute a baby is in her womb,
because you don't want the cycle to continue
and want her to push the agenda of self-love
whilst trying to push through all the comments
she has received,
that deep down she knows are untrue,
but it has been a struggle to subdue
all those thoughts and interactions
that have disturbed her,
imprinted on her psyche like a tattoo.

'I wish I was lighter.'
'I love my skin, but I wish my melanin was brighter.'
'I wish my skin tone was a little bit "whiter".'
I've heard some black girls say.

Oh, how nice it would be

if people were kinder and a bit more sensitive
in their interactions
and through attitudes towards black women,
not being comparative, or negative,
or even expletive.

But
To their doubts, a sedative,
To their beauty, showing lack of prejudice,
and to be fully accepting of their presence.

This Was Never a Place for Us

From when there weren't enough crayons
for us to represent our skin colors
whenever we drew ourselves
we knew this wouldn't necessarily be a place for us.

Education politics

There were always plenty of whites,
and yellows, and pinks
but never enough browns,
blacks, never enough ethnic minority hues

In those drawers in our classrooms
there were always cupboards
bursting of pencils and pens
but there were rarely enough
for us to create our realistic selves

The resentment,
to realise at that age,
That there could never be enough pens
To represent us.

What distress

whilst we were young and this meant nothing to us
this told us that often our narratives
were a victim of erasure.
Our experiences and interactions with education
was often one we'd have to discover undercover.

Education politics

Because how could you ever do
more than *100 years* of black history justice
When it's often condensed into a compression
of minute reconstructions?

We knew there was plenty more out there
than slavery, suffering and dullness
but whenever we always asked for more,
we were always told
"That part's not on the official curriculum.
Those parts don't concern us"
So whenever we asked for minor adjustments
we were told that this would be impossible,
our ideas were shut down with sudden abruptness.

...and so the struggles continued.
Once we were old enough to make curious interruptions,
still these discussions
were laced with questions,
doubts,
assumptions,
so we had to rely on our parents often
to teach us our stories and histories
that at school were always approached with caution.

How heartbreaking for them

to know that all they knew
and all their parents and ancestors told them
were treated as mere options
such history, that was foreign
to many
but because they were discussed in the classroom
they were seen as rotten.

Education politics
continue the cycle of exhaustion.
Our histories, forgotten.
Might be on the curriculum,
but right at the bottom.
If this is ever flagged up, in discussion,
we're suddenly seen as the problem.

Which is why
those initial classroom moments are unforgotten.
The lack of those pencils represented,
an erasure of the history we clutched onto.
How when searching for those brown and black tips
at the back of that cupboard,
we would sometimes struggle.
If only through the lack of those pencils
we could imagine the struggle and trouble
that was unintentionally welcomed
in our minds.

How we could only imagine the dilemmas
these lack of pencils would later represent?

University Storytelling (As An Ethnic Minority)

(Part 1):

As a black woman trying to navigate this space
I feel as if this is not my space.
I feel like i've been misplaced.

Or was I lost?

Because the minute I step into this place,
I feel out of place, displaced.
I'm a fresher, a new face
but the problem is that my face
and the skin colour that indicates my race
will not only affect my price rate,
but also how I feel safe
within these campus walls which feel so small
and make me feel so small (emphasis)

Give me plenty of strength
and a lot more faith
to deal with the microaggressions and bullshit.
 "Can I touch your hair?"
"You must be very familiar with Drake."
And "can we say the n-word?
We know you're black and we're not but trust us,
We don't mean it, we're 'waved', and after all
It's just a phrase."

As a Black woman trying to navigate this space
As a fresher, I'm still trying to find my way
so spare me if I feel a bit weary and a bit dismayed.
I came from London, a multicultural space,
so please excuse me if I feel a delay
feeling comfortable in this place.

As a Black woman trying to navigate this space
Trying to make sense of my degree
and the most of the opportunities around me
so I don't let my 9k go to waste,
but sadly,

there wasn't much that could brace me
for the trials and tribulations that would face me.

I had to flee
my accommodation because
the anxiety my housemates gave me
left me unable to sleep,
and unable to eat.
I told myself I wouldn't let my greatness go to waste
but when you're surrounded by people
who constantly makes accusations due to your race
It makes you exhausted and it makes you feel unwanted.
In your mouth it leaves a fully taste.

So you're stuck between
putting up with the everyday bullshit you face
or calling out people on their disgrace,
but runs the risk of being called 'a bitch',
occasionally a colour accompanying that phrase.

But no names mentioned.

Or did I forget to mention
That representation became fewer
the higher you got with each academic grade.

I'm used to being one of the few black people
In my classes
but please,
don't make me a poster girl
for the whole Black British race.

Because at the end of the day,
I came here to get a degree,
to make my family proud for their sakes.

I haven't 'made' it yet,
I'm still learning about myself,
so please don't make me carry on my shoulders
the weight of both university debt
and the responsibility of 'making it' as a Black woman

into a space that I never possessed.

So please
be easy with me,
I'm just a fresher, a baby girl,

let me settle in with ease.
Check in with me at the end of the degree,
and I'll tell you if I 'made' it,
if I can leave with my degree
and my dignity
whilst simultaneously protecting my peace.

(Part 2; 3 years later as a Masters student)

As a black woman trying to navigate this space
I have now come into my own but
I still deal with the insecurities that I first faced
as a fresh-faced fresher,
full of faith,
becoming suddenly brave.

Congratulations!

You made it through.
You made it through those spaces you considered unsafe
both physically and mentally in your brain.
You made it through those essays
and you navigated people's unknowingly racist ways.

But you still feel a delay
in feeling comfortable in this place.

I've spent 3 years
trying to make the place of my undergraduate
my home.
Now I'm starting again, in a new place.

In this place, I feel an emptiness, a black hole,
questioning:
"How do I start again?
How do I fit in?
What's my role?
How do I make myself feel whole?"

As a Masters student, I'm more self-assured.
I know my goals.
I know what I want to achieve
and I feel as if I'm in a lot more control.

But something inside of me
makes me retreat.
Returning to the fresher I used to be
Insecure in my surroundings and firming

that uneasy feeling in my stomach,
doubting if I'll ever be
the 'successful' Black woman
that people expect of me.

I still feel a delay in feeling
comfortable in this place.

Over 4 months, my hairstyle has changed 4 times.
So much so my lecturer pointed it out
in front of 150+ faces,
pausing the whole lecture to make way
for a sea of eyes turning their heads
to see the new display.

"Black girl in a new place,
Who has changed her hairstyle once again.
Black girl in a new place,
who in under 2 minutes became the talk of the day".

This might appear small in your eyes,
but I won't even lie
I wanted the ground to swallow me up and let me die.
It's as if wherever I go
the microaggressions never leave.
They follow me like fleas,
buzzing doubt in my ears like bees,
paralysing me like a detainee.

As a Black woman trying to navigate this space
Trying to make sense of my degree
and the most of the opportunities around me
so I don't let my 13k fee go to waste
(I'm still broke but in 30 years
all my student debt will be erased)
But sadly,
doing a Masters has cocooned me,
acting as a cushion, a safety net,
until I'm ready to experience the 'real' world's threat.

I'm still expected to have 'made' it
but,
I'm still learning about myself,
so please don't make me carry on my shoulders
the weight of both university debt
and the responsibility of 'making it' as a Black woman
into a space that I never possessed.

It makes me stressed
to know that these feelings won't ever end.
In the workplace,
there's still a strong chance of feeling oppressed
by future bosses, colleagues, partners,

having to suppress
my Blackness in a space
that never made me its guest.

Getting older,
thinking about dating and relationships,
It makes me anxious to know that
Black women appear to only be sexualised
for our bodily features
but are never deemed worthy enough
for meaningful companionships.
It's only when we have large bums and skinny waists
with crazy coca cola shaped hips
that allows us to be deemed worthy
of 'love' that can leave at the click of a switch
but,
our Blackness appears to be a 'barrier'
to experiencing this love
that often comes with conditions
that makes Black women feel
as if they're never enough

"Not too dark, they must be lighter skinned."
"Not too fat, but my girl needs to have a back,
she can't be too thin."

*It's as if Black women can **never** win*

which explains my anxiety and worry
about entering the real world
that gives me pain and stress from within.

So what are my feelings as a Black woman
trying to succeed in this space?
I'm still trying to take things at my own pace,
trying to take each day as it comes,
and bracing myself to deal
with microaggressions and future stresses
with grace.

So please,
be easy with me,
I'm still a student, a baby girl,
let me try and succeed with ease.
Check in with me at the end of this degree
and I'll tell you if I 'made' it,
if I can leave with my degree and my dignity whilst
simultaneously protecting my peace.

What I Would Tell My Daughter

Hands up
Don't shoot

...

is what I would tell my daughter to do.
This is what I would tell my daughter to say,
what I would tell my daughter to do,
is not to be afraid.
Baby girl,
when you're older you will understand
and please don't hate me,
one day you'll understand my words are not in vain.

Hands, hands, hands.

Your hands
that I formed are destined
to perform and transform the world.

Your hands
as maps of growth and molds of me,
your fingers,
your thumbnails,
your wrists and joints preserved.

Baby girl,
understand
your hands will be the function of many things.
I pray you won't ever be using your hands
to beg for your life
convincing those who are meant to protect and serve
you're everything
that your hands are worth saving.
The truth stings but realise that it's for the best,
your hands I created are nothing less than deserving

Hands up, up, up.

When you raise
those hands I formed,
you keep them up, and you don't waver.

Do not sway and do not give way.
Keep those hands up
when you think of their wounds,
and those bullets that shattered their vertebrae,
and those words their mothers pray.
Keep those hands up
even when your heart might be aching,
your nerves might have you shaking.
But Baby girl,
keep them hands up
even when your hope and your strength is fading
and those who are meant
to protect and serve your everything
are degrading
you
and downgrading
you.

Hands up, don't, don't, don't.

Don't limit yourself,

the sky is your limit.
Don't constrict your being.
Do not apologize for your magic.
Do not refuse to resist those oppressive systems
that exist in your world.
Do not remain static.
Love yourself.
Do not treat life as if it is traumatic and full of panic.
Baby girl,
understand that your strength
is as strong as volcanic shockwaves,
your beauty
is as classic as flowers, bouquets and sunshine rays.

Do not let anyone tell you different.
Even those who are meant to
protect and serve your everything,
Who, to your magic are ignorant
and belligerent.
Do not let them be inconsiderate.

Hands up, don't shoot, shoot, shoot.

shoot
bang
execute
attack
gunshot
arrest
physical
cardiac

Young girl,
I pray that one day
you will never experience such an attack
because, and only because, you are Black.

Shoot, hurt.
Authority, asserted.
Power, exerted.

shoot
absolute
brute

Baby girl,
I pray that these gunshots and bullets
will never touch or hurt you.

Hands up, don't shoot.
Hands up, don't shoot.
Hands up, don't shoot.

Don't shoot

Her.
Don't hurt her.
Don't make her life flash before her eyes in a blur.

Don't shoot

those hands.
Don't hurt them.
Don't destroy the hands that I created.

Don't shoot

those hands
that I once cultivated to be celebrated, not mutilated
to be animated, not investigated.

Hands up, ***don't shoot.***

Don't let them shoot your hands.
Baby girl,
This might seem confusing to you,
but I promise, one day, you will understand.

Black Bodies

What are the conversations you've found yourself having about Black bodies? Are they ones of a sexual nature? Or have you been thinking of them to be strong and the athletic type? Are Black bodies still being objectified as they were during the slavery era?

I chose this as a topic for exhibition as I wanted those involved, to show, from their point of view, how they either believed Black bodies were viewed, or how they viewed Black bodies.

Our bodies tend to be looked upon in such sexual ways, and no matter how many times we scream out about it, the topic is still swept aside.

This is an important topic to me and I hope it is to you too. The discussion around what is beautiful and ugly leaves us in difficult places. I can only pray that you think more about the way in which you view your body as a Black person, or how you, as a non-Black, views a Black person's body.

Aaron Daniel, poet for this section, has given poignant points which I believe gives much for us to discuss. He gives us much to ponder upon through his use of words.

Black Bodies

Aaron Daniel

Described by fellow poets as the man with a liquid lexicon, author and spoken word artist Aaron Daniel delivers a form of writing that is layered with ripened fruit beneath the pith. After releasing his first collection of poems 'And Then', with a short story intertwined, pulling the poems together as a sum of parts to form a whole, he is currently working on the release of his highly anticipated second book.

With work filled with introspection and subject matters ranging from love and the essence of being to politics, Aaron Daniel weaves words together to create a beautiful and powerful tapestry displaying his unique perspective of the world.

<u>Grand Rising</u>

Some wear black only for
mourning;
I love that you wear yours as proud adornment.

Some days you dislike your
scars and denounce your
stretch marks; you wish to
call them insecurities but I
have named them Triumph.

Some tomorrows when you tire
of being synonymous with the
strength the world expects yet
somehow still condemns —

My back in broad enough
to hold both of us up for
the times you desire to be
your softest, until the time
you feel ready to recommence.

Untitled

There's a war going on outside...
They say an apple a day keeps
the doctor away; on the day the
democratic Republic of Congo and
Jean Jacques Muyembe sold the
souls of its citizens, agreeing to the
testing of a vaccine for Covid-19
from China, Canada, and the USA.

The pandemonium of pandemics.
The land becoming a laboratory;
I wonder, what will reports say
about the toxicology of dead bodies
made refugees in their own country?
The world continuing to spin on
axis as history repeats; the old story
of Tuskegee in 2020.

Humans have become the
resources and so-called leaders;
custodians complicit in exploiting
the poor have direct hands in
stepfathers raping the motherland

Cassiterite powering our screens,
watching news through calcified
pineal glands —

and the powers that be, relying on
masses to call all conspiracies
theories; revolutionaries sitting in
the prison of a mind that won't
expand.

Branches

How many branches do you have?
Songbirds have flown miles to nest
on the limbs of your lineage as well
as other species less gentle and
more abrasive.

How deep do your roots wander?
I wonder; to what extent they are
willing to stretch your hurt until
from the earth you have been torn
asunder.

Etching their stories in your bark in
attempts to cut you down and
fashion your message into mutters.

Nature's temperate zephyrs play
melodies on your shelter of leaves;
a pleasing relief in a torching
summer.

In awe of how strong you must be;
in spite of everything —
Still providing shade for others

Molala Tree

Gentle zephyrs caressed
black pearls that washed
up on harbours dressed in
scarlet...

At auction, greed came
to dine upon their flesh;
the subjugation of souls
at places hate was made
incarnate.

Where labels placed price tags
for cotton pickers; the thievery
of royalties now chronicled on
parchment paper —

Now property of those who had
bought and mis-sold humanity

...belonging to masters who
      misnamed us for free labour.

But know this young Queen,
young King; you may face
many challenges because of
your skin.

Call on the ancestors
and be reminded of who you were,
before the ships sets sailing,

Before the drowning and all the wailing,
      before the noose;

Before we swung in the breeze
and became strange fruit...

Before the time that you were
                              cut
from your root my Molala tree —

Before the time that you had
forgotten you were powerful.

IMAX

I will live in thy heart, die in thy lap;
no clocking our watches, only
watching each other unconcerned
with time-lapse.

Our frames motion slowly
before quickened to dash;
breaking Coulomb barrier;
your love coming down like
waterfalls, walls collapsed
into splash.

See how our nuclei react;
we land at nerve terminals
marrying spirit with mind
and tapped into synapse
for multi climax...

Cinematic; black gold on silver
screen for our eyes only, moans
surround sound Dolby; pleasure
turned all the way up to IMAX.

Black Hands

Hands can either be seen as threatening or safe spaces. They can be viewed as weapons or as tools to be used for creation. How Black hands are viewed differs based on who the viewer.

Our palms can be read, or we are instructed to raise our hands to where they can be seen when in the presence of authority. In schools, students are told to place their hands on the desks where they can be seen. When growing up we are told to keep our hands to ourselves. Some, when growing up, were meant to feel as though there was something wrong with them if their preferred hand for writing was the left.

If you are like me, you would have previously looked at hands out of curiosity wondering what they have been through and the life of their owner. I am that someone who looks at hands and creates stories about their histories and I wanted to know how someone else would refer to them. It has been interesting to see what Solomon Adams created based on the theme.

Black Hands

Solomon Adams

Solomon Adams is a performance artist and educator. Over the last few years, he has been a strong asset and a respected advocate of London Spoken Word movement where he often collaborates with a variety of established poetry organisations.

As a performance poet, his recent featured performances include performing at the Houses of Parliament, Edinburgh Fringe, Camden Fringe, Leefest, The Ritzy and the re-established Tudor Rose in West London. As a performance artist, he also works in theatre, dance, music production and DJ'ing. A well sought after performer, his soulful and powerful performances have led him to be commissioned by dance company Alleyne Dance and also work alongside Blue Hawk Records in New Jersey, US.

His debut EP, Finding Worlds Again is available on all major platforms.

As an educator, Solomon currently teaches music in West London. He also mentors on an award winning mentoring programme run by the 100 Black Men of London and was recently acknowledged by HM The Queen and Princess Anne for his work in the community. As a poet and a dancer, he also brings his experience working with children delivering spoken word poetry and dance workshops to children around London.

1

The way we mold magic,
The way we materialise melodies,
The way we build empires,
The way we shine ancient,
There is divinity within us,
Guiding our definition,
God's endless love,
A promise that this light always shines
in the darkest of places.

2

Ever had one of those great conversations
with your Uber driver?

Farhan, an East African.
I, a West African.
East and West merge as we travel Central.
His hands placed on the steering wheel,
My hands rested over my baggage,
Our minds joint by a propelling purpose,
Unified by passion proceeding out of us,
This commitment
To our people's liberation and empowerment
On our souls.

We say this work begins here with the end in mind.
To free our people,
We must decolonise our minds,
Must work together
No longer fear what can be taken from us,
Must loosen ourselves from colonial grip,
Must unite strategically to step
Powerfully into the future.

As we approach a Central location,
Emotions take over.
We sense the passion that emanates
From where our hands
Have led us to go this entire time.
The heavens open up hinting
We are better together
Rather than dealing with this alone.

As I depart,
I lay my baggage to the side
that has been held onto for so long.
In releasing them,
Farhan and I embrace
Now having tapped into a radical simplistic truth:
Together we truly do rise.

3

As the sun beats down on this London town,
Shea butter Gods,
Make yourself known
Step into our lives here.
Forgive us for our willingness to leave the house
Without giving our skin
The crème de la crème it deserves.
Lead us not into the hold of ashy ankles
And deliver us from dry skin between our fingers,
For thine is the moisture,
The power and the sun's friend.

Forever and ever,

Ashé.

__4__

Can our Black hands come together
And unite despite whether or not
Our idea of the right path is the same?

5

Struck down again and
Yet still Black hands rise upward.
They can't hold we down.

Black Mental Health

Welcome to a topic with a stigma. Does mental health really affect individuals from the Black community? Is it really just a White person thing? Yes, people within the Black community do have mental health battles, which means only but one thing, it's not *just* a White thing.

Is it spoken about within Black homes? Once upon a time, no, in today's world, it's becoming a topic. Knowledge is key. To understand something opens up room for growth, and growth stems from openness. If families are open for conversations, they are willing to discover more than they had known and impart the knowledge they already have.

This theme needed to be brought up and I thank Georgia for it. In the planning phases for the exhibitions, she suggested that we have Black Mental Heath as a theme and I didn't think twice about it. This was a must.

It's time we come face to face with the topic. We can no longer shy away from it, particularly if we wish for the younger generation to be able to work through their traumas healthily,

Asking Sami to be the poet behind this theme isn't a decision I could ever say I regret. She has touched on topics I know we all need to think about.

I hope you are able to take something from this theme and have the tough conversations which are needed to help you and yours.

Black Mental Health

Sami Rhymes

Sami Rhymes is a Spoken Word Poet & Published Author who also works in project management and as a creative coach. London based and raised. Sami had her first poem published at the age of 9 and has contributed poems to other publications since. 2020 marked the release of her debut poetry collection 20 Something.

Sami has performed, slammed and headlined at a number of public and private events in London and abroad. She has featured on local radio and made her poetry TV debut on the Sky Arts commissioned show Life & Rhymes, hosted by the legendary Benjamin Zephaniah.Sami uses rhyme as a means of release and therapy. Through her spoken word she inspires people in her community to speak up and take action; often addressing taboo topics.

Talking About the Pain

Growing up, I learnt to take the cane
the same way I learnt to take the blame.
Life was never picture perfect,
but I was always getting framed.
A scapegoat, always being blamed.
Detained and defamed in exchange for another's gain.
I knew it was wrong,
but as a child, my tongue was trained
I refrained from talking about pain.
Saying "I'm fine" is a figure of speech programmed
regulated by my brain.
It's easy on the tongue.
But now that I'm older,
it's time for me to undo these wrongs
speak on all the things that went on
when I was young,
before I was born,
and the things that are still going on.
The noise in my head is too strong.
Suffered in silence for too long.
Keep praying I'll crack like cocaine
and pour out the pain
that's been held inside for so long.

Growing up,
I was always told to take things in
be strong,
as if letting things out was so wrong,
told to talk to God or no one,
so if you had no faith you had no one.
Medication was frowned upon
and therapy was talked down on,
so seeking vices to numb pain
is something I really went to town on.

Tried to self-medicate.
Caffeinate,
communicate,

pray,
and even meditate,
but nothing I've tried helps me
to eradicate pain.

So long as I'm breathing; the trauma still remains.
Along with the physical and mental strain of being a
'strong Black woman'.
A role that's far from easy to maintain.
This idea that we're too strong to hurt is insane.
It's time for me
to break away from this conceptual chain.
It's time to get therapy and talk through my pains,
even if it means holding my head down in shame

because I gave Mental Health Services
my family name.
I need to heal, reveal and release this pain.

It's time for me to speak up after years of restraint.
It's time to call out these so-called saints.
These racists, rapists, and oppressors who until this day
keep getting away with their twisted ways.
Just like my ancestors,
I pray and patiently await the day
where justice will be served
and oppressors will be put away.

Now it's time for me to unlearn my learnt ways
and make way for better days.
If I don't change my ways and speak up now,
I'll pass my ways onto my kids
and risk having this cycle of not talking about pain
repeated years down the line from now.

Interracial Therapy

My GP said she's one of the best therapists in the game.
Due to confidentiality he couldn't disclose her name.
Said she was available immediately due to a cancellation
and ready to hear my pains.
I was advised to go with her to avoid playing the waiting game.

She's qualified and looks good on paper
so I assumed she had brains.
Upon meeting, she was very quick to proclaim
that she had experience dealing with females
like me who were BAME.
Only challenge was, our backgrounds weren't the same.
White and privileged.
In society, she holds the reins,
but in therapy, it's not just me that holds the pains.

She tried being professional and humane,
but she's let White Fragility get to her brain.
Shuts me down when I try to open up,
talks over me when I try to explain.
When I bring up racial encounters,
she gets defensive and proclaims
that Paranoia is what is causing me
to make all these claims
and that my experiences
of systemic racism and microaggressions
are completely insane.

In doing so,
she only added to my anxiety,
my trauma,
my anger
and my pain.

       I stopped going to therapy as there was no gain.

She has no idea what it's like
to walk a mile in my lane.
To carry my Black skin,
Black body,
and Black name.
To be fat shamed for having a Black frame
and called names
like 'blick', 'drop lip' and 'monkey' all day.
Fetishised and portrayed in the wrong way.
Experiencing abuse in all ways
from a young age.
At school and in the workplace,
discriminated for my race.
Brought down by racists in high places.
Pulled up by police in the streets and on highways.

Having weapons shoved in my face.
Cuffed and touched all over the place.
Without consent.
I've been hurt.
I'm not content but I'm hellbent on healing.
I just need to find a Black female therapist
who can relate to how I'm feeling.

Being Black's a Crime

There's no sugar in this cane.
Don't mind a bit of pain,
but being whipped and stripped ain't the same
when you're being restrained and detained
for a crime you didn't commit.
Matching a description
that only your skin colour seems to fit.
Being Black's the crime for which they want to convict.

Innocent until proven guilty,
but in their eyes Black is filthy
and you're guilty until proven innocent.
Prison is imminent and once you're inside
these prison guards move militant.
Multiple participants
caught up in an array of incidents.
Reports of broken limbs and torn ligaments.
Beaten like an instrument.
Witnesses silenced.
No one was vigilant.
Malfunctioning bodycams.

What a coincidence?!

Too many Blacks caught up
in similar predicaments.
All of this is equivalent
to cases of false imprisonment
and cases where officers
have been responsible for planting weapons
and stimulants.
Adults taken in
generally face 5-10 years of imprisonment.
Some are given life;
5 years is typically the minimum sentence
given to young males that are Black and innocent.
White offenders plead guilty to the same crimes

yet manage to get off with
"insufficient evidence"
The racial disparity in the criminal justice system
is evident.
Richard Phillips spent over 45 years
incarcerated in the state of Michigan.
Wrongfully convicted of murder
despite having long proclaimed his innocence.
Eventually exonerated in 2018
when the man responsible for the crime came forward
supplying new evidence.
Meanwhile innocent bros on death row
lay on their knees
praying prosecutors find new evidence.

They are trying to get rid of all the Black citizens.
From Western born to first-generation immigrants

and the attempts to annihilate us are getting ridiculous.
They even stop and search us to ridicule us.
Then arrest us for resisting them
even when it's clear that we ain't resisting them.
Mentally sick of them.
Physically can't deal with them.
Any form of contact literally
seems to trigger hypervigilance.

Mentally sore.
Flashbacks of things that we saw
when made to feel sore.
Anxiety sores and the impact of the trauma is raw.
Can't even hug loved ones anymore.
Constantly at war.
Fighting for a free mind
and a trauma-free life.
There's more to being free than walking freely outside.
Putting us inside has messed us up inside,
the direct impact of being incarcerated
and institutionalised.

A prisoner in this life
and a prisoner in our minds,
doing time for being a particular kind of kind.

We have our movement restricted
until proven innocent and acquitted.
Only to be released into the same
racist society from which we were omitted.
It's never too long
before we hear of another Black soul that's been killed
or wrongfully convicted.
Hospitalised or readmitted.
Sectioned for not being with it.
Attempts of suicide cos the mind feels rigid.
Carrying involuntary memories of trauma so vivid.
Never feeling free.
Constantly having to relive it.
Racially profiled.
Until death comes,
we have to live with it.
These White supremacists
and bigots hate to admit it
but being born Black
is the only crime that's being committed.

Black Don't Crack

They say Black don't crack, but we sure do fall apart.
Broken homes, broken bones, and broken hearts.
Just like cars, we've broken down and lost some parts.
Lost minds. Lost souls. Lost limbs.
We've watched all these things depart
like loved ones.
One way or another we've been torn apart
and the system has played its part.

We've been victims of the darkest of arts.
Had it hard from the start.
Born Black so we know better than anyone
what it feels like to be dark,
so much so that we try keeping people in the dark
when things go wrong and we get wronged.
Tell ourselves we're independent and don't need anyone.
Programmed to be tough and built to stand strong.
Hold it together even when tired of holding on.

They're tired of our skin, yet they bathe in the sun.
They heard we don't age so they take us when young.
Keep us in chains with nowhere to run.
Put us behind bars and take us with guns.
Put us in chokeholds and kill us for fun.
Have us enduring pain until we are numb.
But we can't cry. It's considered wrong.
We can't crack. As Black's we must be strong.

Dynamics in the Black Family

To the younger generation, this is the conversation we've been longing for. For the older generation, this may be a touch and go subject.

In today's world, we, I guess I speak for the younger generation, have been trying to find methods to unlearn some of the things we learnt growing up. It's not been very easy for some of us and based on our parents' upbringings, we've had to cope with the way they chose to bring us up.

I must once again thank Georgia for suggesting this theme. As this was her suggestion, and my wanting her to be apart of this project, I couldn't give this to anyone else but her.

What she has put together for you all, is more than just poetry. Georgia chose to write an essay to best address further themes under the umbrella of *Dynamics in the Black Family*.

I believe this is a key topic when it comes to talking about The Black Experience. We are who we are because of our upbringing. We respond the way we do, because of our upbringing.

For us to go forward and empower the younger generation, these points need to be addressed. To progress in a healthy manner, we need to take heed, if needs be, seek counselling as to stop from putting our children through the things we went through within our homes.

Dynamics in the Black Family

Georgia Moona-Sam

Georgia is an aspiring and budding writer, trying different mediums of writing on her journey as a multi-faceted writer, not only is she currently learning new styles she has also written for a local Zine back in 2016, touching upon a subject around racial politics within the school system in the UK. Currently, Georgia is currently writing something for an original idea and has had previous work put up in an art gallery.

Toxicity in the Black Community
A Somewhat Educated Rant

The purpose of this isn't to shame, scold, disrespect, or ridicule the Black community. I am simply looking at and dissecting certain attributes pertaining to parental patterns and behaviours which are damaging in some cases and respects. With that being said, let's begin.

Lack Of Openness

In my research of this wide and broad topic, I came across the lack of openness which means, more often than not, that a lot of our young Black people and adults (aged 16 - mid 20s) feel like they cannot find comfort in speaking to their parents or respective carers. I find that it usually starts from a young age, usually when you start becoming more inquisitive and curious about life; I remember being young and asking my Mum or Dad about something on TV and getting: *"I don't know"*, *"mind your business"*, or simply *"ask your Mum/Dad"* as a meagre response. As a child, you tend to brush these factors off due to it just being childish rantings.

The link to be made with this is, when you become much older (let's say teen years) and your questions develop into things about structure and maybe even sometimes questioning an adult, you tend to be made out as *"disrespectful"*, *"mouthy"*, *"rude"*, or *"out of line"* to name a few. This subsequently leads the young person to feel as if their voice isn't something that is desired to be heard, which can be linked to this lack of openness. Young individuals feel like they cannot be open inside (and sometimes outside) the home, leaving the parent last to understand what is going on with their child if they can't communicate with their parent.

Another point I want to raise is that a child or young person is disregarded or not heard when they come forth with an issue or has yet to explain themselves, whether it be about something they've been made responsible for, or them saying their side of a story. Often, when this happens, the child's side will be left unknown or not believed **because** they are a child. This way of thinking makes no sense; distrust due to their age does not make their side invalid. For example, a child has had a run in with their teacher at school and the parent will believe the teacher's word over the child which leads to meaningless and pointless punishment. On the other hand, there are also parents out there who think they know their child and regardless if the child is right or wrong, the parent will persist with the impression that their child is "an angel".

Moreover, to solidify this point, a lot of the time the treatment of young Black girls verses young Black boys is old and Draconian; the very fact that in this day and age we're still treating our sons better than our daughters is odd to me, exemplified by the topic of treatment of boys and girls, to which will be expanded on later.

To bring this section to a close, I return to the idea of pointless punishment without meaningful cause, which is associated with one another in the sense of publicly embarrassing, humiliating or ridiculing a child. Trying to take control of the situation by attempting to make an example of the child is just like shouting your business in public; It's not productive and the child will just feel like a laughing stock. With the rise of social media, my point is being constantly reiterated under the guise of cheap Instagram entertainment.

Treatment Female and Male Children

In this part of the essay, I'll be looking deeper into the treatment of female and male children within the Black household. I understand that with this argument that it can go both ways in respect of, male siblings getting better treatment than their female siblings and vice versa; so I'll try my best to look at both sides of the coin.

With the research I've done and speaking to a few individuals, I've seen that this is something that a lot of the Black youth and community experience.

I understand that in some respects there are cultures where this is the default, but somewhere along the line we must question the inclusivity of these "traditions". Female siblings are raised under more control; who they can be friends with, who they chose to date, and once they do date HOW they are to date. For example, a friend of mine was told that she mustn't tell any of her future partners about her academic accolades in fear of "intimidating" her partner. Now, in this day and age the playing field is more level in the respect of men feeling intimidated by well educated women, my personal opinion. I feel men of this age are more attracted to that especially Black men, so now I feel like it's time to change that narrative of telling girls they must hide who they because others may feel "intimidated" by them.

Stories we're all too familiar with: *"I was the Black sheep of the family"* and *"my parents charged me rent but not my older/younger brother"*. The problems with this are a mixed bag; first being the fact that usually with this dynamic, several rifts between are created between the parent(s) and their kid. Between the kids it's more than just sibling rivalry. Favouritism creates almost a sort of dislike from one sibling to the other because they feel not as important as the favoured one.

Onto the flipside; female siblings being treated better than the male sibling. In some respects, there's a sense of disconnect between the dynamic of the family whether it be mother, daughter, and son, or a whole family unit where the father is present. In this example I'm using, the dynamic of which the father isn't present. So in this perspective the male sibling doesn't have anyone HE FEELS he cannot rely or talk to about issues he is battling with, so it forces him to seek validation from family members (which there is nothing wrong with) or people outside the home. Sometimes it can also be a result of comparing them to each other which again creates this rift of which is often filled with a sense of animosity between the two.

To conclude this somewhat educated rant, I'd like to reiterate that the purpose of this piece isn't to divide or cause a ruffle in the community, these are just pinpoints of a few truths, I and many others have either come across or experienced. We need to be able to heal and take into consideration that we are not our parents and we deserve respect and nurturing. In a way for our generation to understand our own upbringing we must be able to take these factors and issues and change the narrative of toxic parenting within our community.

Final Remarks

I cannot thank you enough for buying a copy of this book. I hope you've not only found the entertainment value in it, but you've also gained from it.

I think it's so difficult to explain to others what it's like being Black, but I do believe the poets who took part in sharing their art and heart with you, were able to eloquently do so.

This is only the first Volume of the It Will Be anthologies. There will be more to come where different themes will be explored.

On that note, if you wish to be published in one of the upcoming volumes, do get in touch and we can put something together.

The upcoming volumes are:

His Point of View
Her Mind, Her Voice
This Muslim's Reality
Overcomers

Our email address is info@4dhouseltd.com, if you believe this is something you'd be interested in writing for, feel free to send us an email.

How to Further Support

We are on Instagram as @4dhouseltd and our website is www.4dhouseltd.com. If you would like to contact us, our email address is info@4dhouseltd.com.

Please do leave a review for us on Amazon. As this book was independently published, we need your reviews to allow others to see it on Amazon. Help us to share the work of these poets with those out of our standard circle.

To keep up with the poets, please do follow them and share their pages and works with your friends and family.

Tiri The Seed - IG @tiritheseed
Alex Otubanjo - IG @alexotubanjooo
AMD Speaks - IG @official_amd_speaks
Solomon Adams - IG @solomonssoul
SamiRhymes - IG @samirhymes
Georgia Moona-Sam - TikTok @SamOnTheMoon

www.ingramcontent.com/pod-product-compliance
Lightning Source LLC
Chambersburg PA
CBHW061224070526
44584CB00029B/3977